BEAUTIFUL DERBYSHIRE

A long, narrow county stretching nort... the outskirts of Manchester, Derbysh... spectacular and varied scenery in Engla... market towns and spas, delightful stone-built villages... churches and stately homes. The scenery varies from the peat moor-land and precipitous gritstone rock faces of the sombre High, or Dark, Peak to the gentler Low, or White, Peak which is known for its unspoilt valleys and meandering rivers. Established as Britain's first national park in 1951, the Peak District is often regarded as synonymous with Derbyshire although it covers only about a third of the county. Derbyshire also has a fascinating history for the southern lowlands were one of the cradles of the industrial revolution, famous for the production of textiles and fine china, and Derby itself was the centre of a large railway network.

High Neb, Stanage Edge

Pickering Tor, Dovedale

DOVEDALE The Derbyshire Dales are many and varied in their size and scenery but, without doubt, the best known and most visited is Dovedale. Here the picturesque River Dove meanders between wooded slopes and limestone outcrops. To admire its many splendours the visitor can follow the river upstream on foot to the hamlet of Milldale and on up through Beresford Dale and Wolfscote Dale to Hartington.

Dominating the entrance to the dale is massive Thorpe Cloud below which a line of stepping stones crosses the river. Among the famous natural features of Dovedale is the tall pinnacle of Ilam Rock, with Pickering Tor in attendance. The village church at Ilam has a number of Saxon crosses and above Ilam Rock are many well-known attractions including Lion Rock, Reynards Cave, Tissington Spires, Lovers Leap and the Dove Holes.

At the head of the dale the Dove passes through narrows known as the Nabs – above is Milldale. Here the stream is crossed by an ancient pack-horse bridge. Further upstream above Wolfscote Dale the picturesque village of Hartington has a fine medieval church and cottages grouped around a duck pond.

Thorpe Cloud, Dovedale

The Duck Pond, Hartington

Milldale Village

High Street, Ashbourne

ASHBOURNE   The pleasant market town of Ashbourne is the southern gateway to the Dales and the stepping off point for visits to Dovedale. There is a fine church, known as the "Pride of the Peak", and in the centre of the town the distinctive "gallows" sign of the Green Man Inn spans the street.

Parish Church, Ashbourne

Well-Dressing A custom unique to Derbyshire, well-dressing is reputed to have started in the village of Tissington. It involves decorating the wells with colourful pictures comprised of flower petals representing scenes both traditional and modern. The custom began as a thanksgiving to God for the continued supply of water, the root of all life and fertility. Tissington has five wells that in times of draught have never failed and during the great plague of 1665 to 1666 reputedly kept the village free from infection by the purity of their water.

TISSINGTON The village of Tissington is undoubtedly one of the most picturesque in Derbyshire and has a more rural setting than places further north in the Peak District. The duck pond, stone cottages and Tudor Hall – seat of the Fitzherberts – combine to present a delightful picture. Tissington is particularly known for its well dressing when the five wells around the village are decorated with Biblical pictures.

Heights of Abraham Cable Railway

North Parade, Matlock Bath

Grand Pavilion, Matlock Bath

THE MATLOCKS The town of Matlock, with attendant Matlock Bath, lies on the River Derwent. Matlock's heyday was as a spa town in the nineteenth and early twentieth centuries and its Regency and Victorian architecture are a reminder of this past popularity. The Hydro was opened in 1853, creation of John Smedley – on a hill above the town is the home he had built for himself, castellated Riber Castle.

Today Matlock is a centre for exploring the southern Peak District and is set amongst fine scenery. Between Matlock and Matlock Bath the Derwent passes High Tor, a 400 feet high cliff rising precipitously from the river.

On the opposite side are the Heights of Abraham, probably named after the battlefield of Quebec in 1759. A path leads to the top but today an easier route is afforded by a modern cable railway. Apart from the fine views the Heights is famous for its caves.

In Matlock Bath a riverside walk runs the length of North and South Parades and the dominant feature beside the Derwent is the Grand Pavilion.

Hall Ley's Park, Matlock

High Tor and Matlock

Parish Church, Chesterfield

CHESTERFIELD This busy modern town has grown up on the site of Saxon and Roman settlements. It is best known today for the remarkable crooked 14th century spire on the Parish Church of St. Mary and All Saints. It is thought that the malformation of the 228 feet high octagonal spire was caused by the use of unseasoned timber, allowing the wooden frame to warp. Among Chesterfield's other historic buildings are the Royal Oak Inn in The Shambles, which dates from Tudor times, and a fine Georgian terrace in Saltergate.

DERBY The Romans also had a camp at Derby which became a busy market town in Norman times. With the coming of the industrial revolution it developed into a manufacturing centre and England's first silk mill was established here in 1717. The mill now houses a museum of industrial archaeology and its gates are one of the best examples of wrought-iron work in Britain. There are many fine buildings, old and new, in the town. These include the elegant Council House beside the River Derwent. On the 18th century bridge which crosses the river is a rare bridge chapel dedicated to St. Mary which dates from the 1300s.

River Derwent and Old Council House, Derby

Hardwick Hall

Kedleston Hall

HARDWICK HALL Noted for the size and number of its windows, Hardwick Hall was built in 1597 for Elizabeth Shrewsbury, Bess of Hardwick. Her initials are incorporated in the decorative stonework on the top of the huge towers at each corner. The house contains many fine Tudor portraits and an outstanding collection of tapestries and needlework.

KEDLESTON HALL Surrounded by a 500-acre park, Kedleston Hall is one of the greatest achievements of the 18th century designer Robert Adam. Commissioned by the Curzon family this splendid mansion has a magnificent marble hall and state rooms. An Indian Museum houses objects collected when he was Viceroy of India by Lord Curzon.

Haddon Hall from the River Wye

HADDON HALL   In a romantic wooded setting above the River Wye is Haddon Hall, the oldest and most charming of the great Derbyshire houses. With its battlemented walls and towers it is a fine example of a medieval fortified manor house – perhaps the finest in England. The Norman chapel is exquisite and the domestic rooms have altered little since Tudor times. The attractive terraced courtyard garden is also a feature.

CHATSWORTH HOUSE   One of the greatest of English stately homes is magnificent Chatsworth, in its idyllic setting beside the River Derwent. Seat of the Dukes of Devonshire, the house dates from 1550, the present exterior being late 17th century. The interior contains a wealth of treasures and spectacular state rooms – the park was laid out by Capability Brown and the formal gardens by Sir Joseph Paxton.

Paxton also designed the nearby "model village" of **Edensor,** built in the mid 19th century for estate workers.

Edensor Village

Chatsworth House

BAKEWELL · At the heart of the Peak District is Bakewell, an historic little town of quiet streets and ancient houses. The fine stone bridge, dating from around 1300, is one of the oldest in England, and the impressive central-spired church contains a chapel to the Vernons of Haddon Hall. The famous Bakewell Pudding originated in the town and the Old Original Bakewell Pudding Shop can be patronised.

Parish Church, Bakewell

The Square, Bakewell

Eyam Hall and Stocks

EYAM To the north of Bakewell lies the plague village of Eyam, so named because the Great Plague of 1665 decimated the local population. Only 90 from some 350 inhabitants survived. Despite this grim past it is a pretty place with picturesque cottages and a fine old Hall, which dates from 1676.

Plague Cottages, Eyam

Monsal Dale from Monsal Head

THE RIVER WYE Above Bakewell the clear waters of the River Wye pass through three beautiful dales – Chee Dale, Millers Dale and Monsal Dale. Highest is rugged Chee Dale, dominated on its northern side by the cliffs of Chee Tor, a popular spot for climbers. Millers Dale also has limestone cliffs but is more wooded and sylvan and offers excellent fishing.

Monsal Dale is the longest and most accessible of the three dales. From the escarpment of Monsal Head there is a fine view across the dale – although man-made the railway viaduct seems to add to the impressiveness of the aspect.

Below Monsal Dale the Wye flows past **Ashford-in-the-Water** with its two ancient bridges. Sheepwash Bridge creates a particular idyllic scene.

To the north of Millers Dale, on the uplands, is the large village of Tideswell with its finely proportioned medieval parish church, known locally as the "Cathedral of the Peak". The village has a long history having been granted a market charter as far back as 1250.

Sheepwash Bridge

Monsal Dale

Miller's Dale

The River Wye, Miller's Dale

In Chee Dale

Church and Square, Tideswell

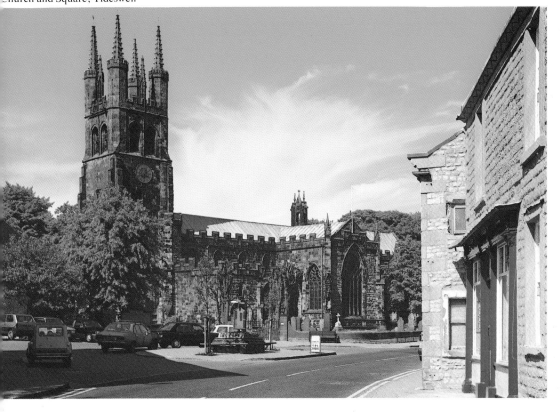

The River Wye, Pavilion Gardens, Buxton

Pavilion Gardens, Buxton

Buxton from the Town Hall

BUXTON The spa town of Buxton lies on the fringe of the High Peak and is noted for its fine grey stone Georgian and Regency architecture. Centre of the town is the classically proportioned Crescent, designed in 1780. The impressive Royal Devonshire Hospital is reputed to have the largest dome in Europe. The Pump Room, Thermal Baths and St. Annes Well all date from the heyday of the town's popularity in the nineteenth century.

The River Wye flows through Buxton and it has been attractively landscaped where it passes through the Pavilion Gardens and along the Serpentine Walk. Within the gardens the glass-domed Pavilion is the venue for events throughout the year.

Outside Buxton on the Macclesfield road is the well known Cat and Fiddle Inn, second highest public house in England, often exposed to the wilds of winter weather. Also close by is the picturesque Vale of Goyt.

Vale of Goyt

Cat and Fiddle Inn

Cavedale and Peveril Castle, Castleton

Winnats Pass

Peveril Castle and Mam Tor

CASTLETON Set in the heart of the High Peak Castleton is surely one of the most impressively situated and unique villages in England. Visitors are drawn to the place for its spectacular scenery, medieval castle and fabulous caverns.

Dominating the village are the ruins of Peveril Castle, an early Norman fortress begun by William Peverel, one of William the Conqueror's trusted knights. Although now ruined it is well worth the strenuous climb if only for the splendid views. To the south-west is the massive sculptured form of Mam Tor, the "Shivering Mountain". This is so-named because its rock face is gradually weathering away and changing shape. Further to the south the Buxton road plunges between the limestone cliffs of the Winnats Pass, famous for its grim murder story of two young lovers done to death by local miners in 1758.

The real wonder of Castleton is its four caverns, each with spectacular galleries and chambers. The Blue John Mine yields the beautiful Blue John spar, fashioned into delicate ornaments, and the Great Hall of the Speedwell Cavern is reached by boat along a flooded mineshaft.

Square and Castle, Castleton

Castleton from above

Pennine Way, Edale

THE HIGH PEAK The northern part of Derbyshire is taken up by a wild and wind-swept landscape, the countryside of the High Peak. In fact there are no peaks but the majority of the moorland lies around the 2,000 feet contour. Highest point is Kinder Scout (2,088 feet) and for the walk to the summit the best starting off point is the hamlet of Edale. The Pennine Way follows the line of the dale itself.

The Peak itself is only crossed by one road, the main Sheffield to Glossop route, which cuts through the impressive Snake Pass, often snowed up in winter. To the west of the pass the road skirts one arm of the Ladybower Reservoir, the largest in England when opened in 1945. This the lowest of the three reservoirs, formed by the damming of the River Derwent, and which make up a Derbyshire "Lake District".

Particularly imposing, in a wooded setting, is the stone built Derwent Dam with its twin towers. This dam was used for practice by the Dambusters squadron before its famous Second World War raid on the Ruhr dams.

Snake Pass

Derwent Dam

Ladybower Reservoir

THE PEAK DISTRICT
AND NORTH MIDLANDS.

Printed and Published by
J. Salmon Ltd., Sevenoaks, Kent ©